SIXTH CLASS PUPIL'S BOOK

Switch on Science

Clíona Murphy • Helena Jeffrey

Carroll Heinemann
Units 17-18
Willow Road Business Park
Knockmitten Lane
Dublin 12
http://www.carrollheinemann.ie

Copyright © Clíona Murphy and Helena Jeffrey, 2004
Managing Editor: Maggie Greaney
Designer: Jackie Hill, 320 Design
Artwork: Shelagh McNicholas and Ian Lusted

First published April 2004

ISBN 1 84450 002 0

Photo acknowledgements
Bubbles p 29 (attic insulation); Camera Press Ireland p 12 (icicles on roof); David Wootton
Photography pp 38 (bluebell covered woodland), 58 (windsurfer); Ecoscene pp 11 (car wash),
16 (helium balloons), 29 (wall insulation), 39 (earthworm & bladderwrack), 47 (person with
microscope), 55 (dentist with drill), 58 (hydraulic lift & ship); Imagefile Ireland pp 11 (boiling
kettle), 12 (steaming pot of water, washing on line & condensation on window), 16 (neon
sign, fire extinguisher & soft drinks can), 38 (bluebell), 39 (garden snail), 47 (human eye), 55
(pneumatic drill & car tyre), 58 (kite); Images Colour Library (tree frog icon); Last Resort
Picture Library pp 47 (camera), 58 (car on garage platform); PhotoDisc pp (planet icon, light
bulb icon & clothes peg icon); PPL Limited pp 9 (wind instruments); 11 (Greg Collins/person
drinking water), 16 (Greg Collins/gas ring), 29 (Greg Collins/double-glazed window), 55 (Greg
Collins/pneumatic wrench); The Irish Image Collection pp 58 (digger, refuse truck and water
wheel)

Cover acknowledgements
Alamy Images (light bulbs); PhotoDisc (light bulb)

Contents

Food in our bodies and staying healthy

Draw what you think happens to food and drink inside your body.
Label each part.

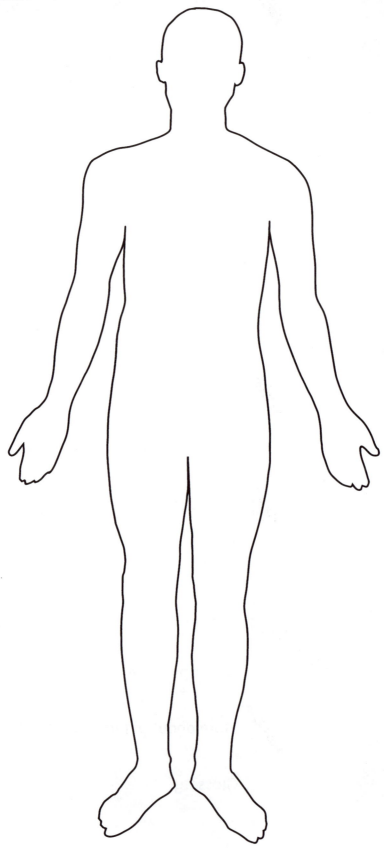

Discuss with your partner what happens to food we eat.

Food in our bodies and staying healthy

The digestive system

When we eat, the pieces of food we swallow are too big to be absorbed into our bodies. They are broken down into tiny pieces so they can be taken around our body by the blood. This takes place in our **digestive system**.

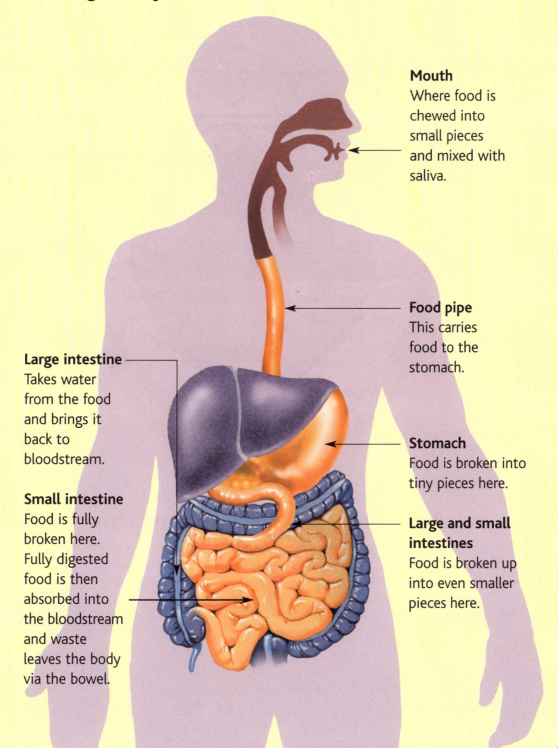

Mouth
Where food is chewed into small pieces and mixed with saliva.

Food pipe
This carries food to the stomach.

Stomach
Food is broken into tiny pieces here.

Large and small intestines
Food is broken up into even smaller pieces here.

Large intestine
Takes water from the food and brings it back to bloodstream.

Small intestine
Food is fully broken here. Fully digested food is then absorbed into the bloodstream and waste leaves the body via the bowel.

Food in our bodies and staying healthy

Teeth are part of the digestive system. We have different types of teeth that do different jobs. Can you remember the names of the different types of teeth? Write them in.

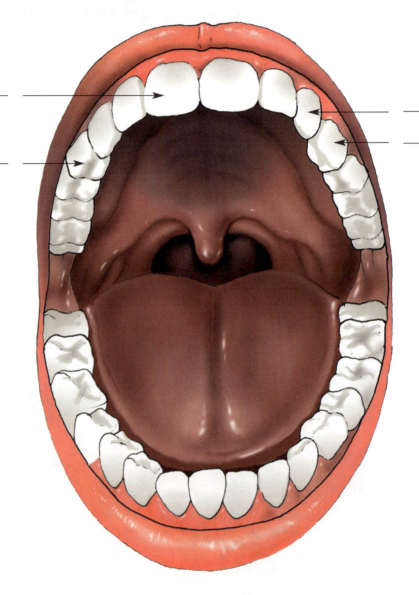

What are our different teeth used for? Record your answers here.

Type of tooth	What it is used for

Food in our bodies and staying healthy

Structure of a tooth

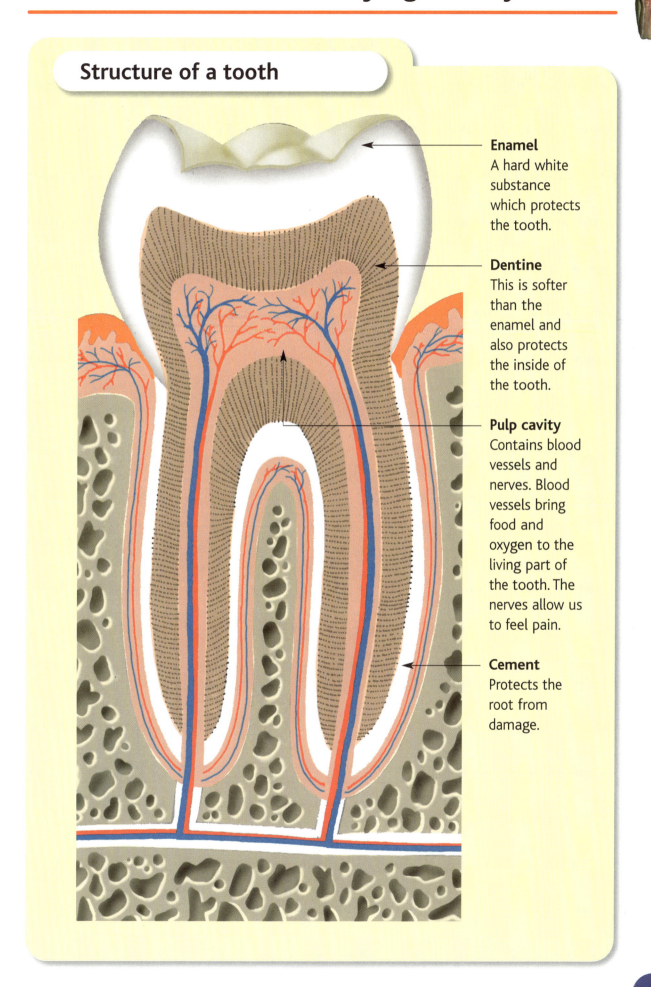

Enamel
A hard white substance which protects the tooth.

Dentine
This is softer than the enamel and also protects the inside of the tooth.

Pulp cavity
Contains blood vessels and nerves. Blood vessels bring food and oxygen to the living part of the tooth. The nerves allow us to feel pain.

Cement
Protects the root from damage.

Food in our bodies and staying healthy

Draw diagrams of things we can do that keep healthy and things that make us unhealthy.

Food in our bodies and staying healthy

Do you remember food groups?

Fats
Fats are found in cheese, butter, oil, biscuits and sweets. Fats give us energy and help keep our bodies warm.

Calcium
Calcium is found in dairy products like milk and cheese. Calcium is a very important mineral. It keeps our bones and teeth strong.

Vitamins
Vitamins are found in fruit and vegetables. They are important for healthy bones, teeth and skin. Vitamins are also good for our eyesight.

Proteins
Proteins are found in foods such as meat, fish, dairy products and nuts. Proteins are essential for our bodies to grow. Proteins also help repair or replace worn out parts of the body.

Iron
Iron is found in red meats and green leafy vegetables. Iron is another very important mineral. It helps keep our blood healthy.

Carbohydrates
Carbohydrates are found in bread, potatoes, rice and pasta. Carbohydrates give us energy to do things.

The sound of music

How sound is made

Sound is produced when something **vibrates**. Most vibrations are too fast for the eye to see. We can feel vibrations of many sounds. If you put your hand on a radio when it is switched on, you can feel the vibrations. Banging, shaking, plucking elastic bands or tapping glass bottles all cause the air around them to vibrate.

The sound of music

Make a kazoo.

You will need
- greaseproof paper
- kitchen roll tube
- elastic band

What to do

1 Place the greaseproof paper over the end of the tube. Hold it in place with the elastic band. Describe the sound it makes when you hum into it.

_____

2 Hum into the other end. Describe the sound it makes.

_____

3 Make longer and shorter kazoos. Hum into them. What happens to the sound when you change the length of the kazoo?

_____

_____

Make a drinking straw oboe.

You will need
- plastic straws
- scissors

What to do
- Pinch one end of the straw between your thumb and forefinger to flatten it.
- Cut off the flattened corners so it looks like a sharpened pencil.
- Put about 2.5cm of the cut straw end into your mouth. (Keep your lips closed but not tightly.)
- Rest the straw on your lower teeth. Blow hard into the straw. If there is no sound, blow less hard until a sound is made.
- Make the straw shorter by cutting the end of it, or make it longer by joining another straw of the same size to the first straw.

1 What happens to the sound when you change the length of the straw?

_____

_____

The sound of music

Wind instruments

Wind instruments are made from wooden or metal pipes. The pipes produce sounds when the air inside vibrates. This happens when the musician blows into the instrument. The length of vibrating air inside the pipe is called the air column. Sounds are produced when this air vibrates. The pipes also contain holes, where the musicians place their fingers. The length of the air column inside can be made shorter or longer depending on how many finger holes the musician covers. This is how notes of different pitches (high or low) are made - the shorter the air column the higher the **pitch**.

The sound of music

How we hear

Ear flap
Sends sound waves into the inner ear.

Hammer, anvil, stirrup
Three little bones that pick up the vibrations and pass them to the cochlea.

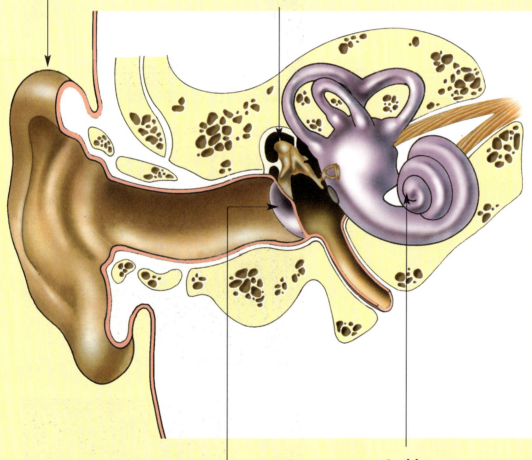

Ear drum
Sound waves cause the ear drum to vibrate.

Cochlea
Changes the vibrations into messages which are passed along the nerves to the brain. The brain makes sense of the messages and we 'hear' the sounds.

Changing materials

Water

Water is necessary for life. Humans may survive for weeks without food but would die without water after a few days.

Washing, cooking, cleaning and some sporting activities also require water.

Industries use huge quantities of water. The manufacture of paper, steel, rubber and chemicals depends on a water supply.

About 71% of the earth's crust is covered with water. Fresh water is found in rivers, lakes and reservoirs.

Water is a liquid at room temperature. At 0°C it freezes and becomes solid.

When water is heated, it evaporates and becomes an invisible gas called water vapour. Water boils at 100 °C.

Changing materials

Write what has happened to the water in each picture. Use the word bank to help you.

_____

_____

_____

_____

boiling   condensing   melting   freezing   evaporating

Write the correct word on each arrow.

solid   ⟶   liquid   ⟶   gas

        ⟵   ⟵

Changing materials

Sort the changes that are taking place.

Change	Description of change	New materials made (yes/no)	Permanent or temporary change?
frying egg			
toast			
chocolate melting			
vitamin C tablet fizzing in a glass			
burning candle			
sugar dissolving in water			
clay being fired in a kiln			
metal melting			
concrete setting			
puddle freezing			
car rusting			

13

Properties and characteristics of materials

Write what happened in each case.

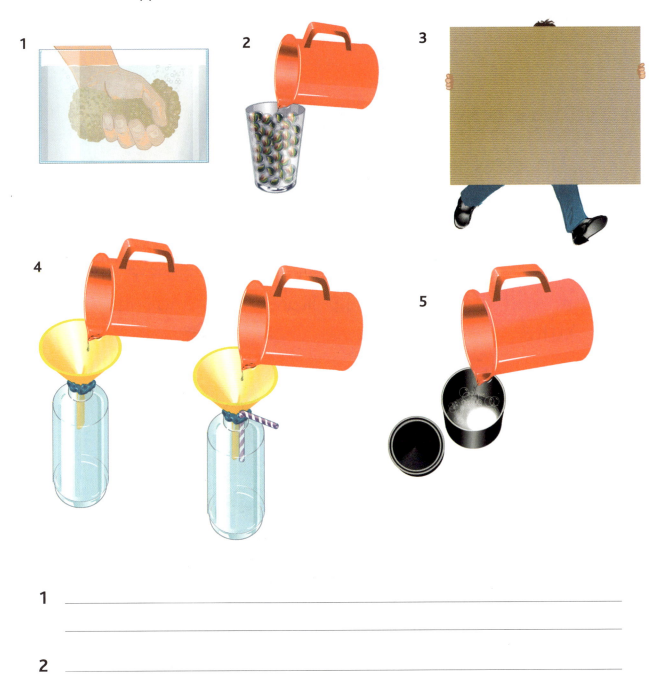

1 _____
_____

2 _____
_____

3 _____
_____

4 _____
_____

5 _____
_____

Properties and characteristics of materials

This is Know-It-All Neil. He thinks he knows everything. Read what he thinks about air. Talk to your Switch on Science investigators. Then write Neil a reply to convince him that air exists.

Dear SoS Investigators,

Air does not exist. It has no smell. I cannot touch it and I cannot see it even though my eyesight is excellent.

If I cannot see it then I don't believe it. It will take a lot to make me change my mind.

Yours Sincerely,
Neil

Properties and characteristics of materials

For you to find out.

There are lots of different gases. Some gases can be very useful.

Which gas is used to keep these balloons in the air?

Which gas is used to light up this sign?

Which gas is used in this fire extinguisher?

Which gas is used to make this cooker work?

Which gas is used to put the fizz in this drink?

Air

Air is all around us. Air is a mixture of different gases. The three main gases in air are oxygen (20%), nitrogen (78%) and carbon dioxide (3 - 4%). Because we cannot see them, it is difficult to understand this. If you could see air it might look like this.

All fall down

Gravity

1 a Which ball do you think will fall to the ground first?

_____

b Which fell to the ground first. Why?

_____

_____

2 Are the children carrying out a fair test? Why?

_____

_____

_____

_____

_____

3 a Which piece of paper do you think will hit the ground first? Why?

_____

_____

b Which hit the ground first? Why?

_____

_____

4 Which parachute do you think will stay in the air for longer? Why?

_____

_____

_____

_____

_____

All fall down

Gravity

Gravity is the force that pulls everything towards the centre of the earth. If you throw a ball in the air, gravity is what makes it fall back down again. If you jump off a wall, gravity will always pull you towards the ground. Isaac Newton discovered gravity. According to a story, he was sitting under a tree when an apple hit him on the head. He wondered why it fell downwards and not off in any other direction. He thought about this and realised that there is a force pulling everything towards the centre of the earth. This force is gravity.

Draw four diagrams to show how gravity pulls everything towards the centre of the earth. Write a sentence to explain what gravity is doing in each case.

All fall down

Mass and weight

There is a difference between the **mass** and **weight** of something. The mass of something is not a force. The mass of something is how much matter or material it contains or, to put it more simply, a measure of how difficult it is to move. Mass is measured in kilograms. The mass of something never changes wherever it is. The weight of something does change depending on where it is.

The force of gravity is weaker on the moon. If you were to go to the moon you would weigh less but your mass would stay the same. The weight of an astronaut on the moon is about one-sixth of his or her weight on earth. In deep space, your weight would be zero because there is no gravity there. Weight is a force, measured in newtons (N).

A weighing scales measures how much an object is being pulled by gravity. Measure the weight of different objects in your classroom. Record your measurements here.

What I measured	What it weighed

All fall down

Which child do you agree or disagree with? Why?

I agree with _____ because _____

_____

I disagree with _____ because _____

_____

Its electric!

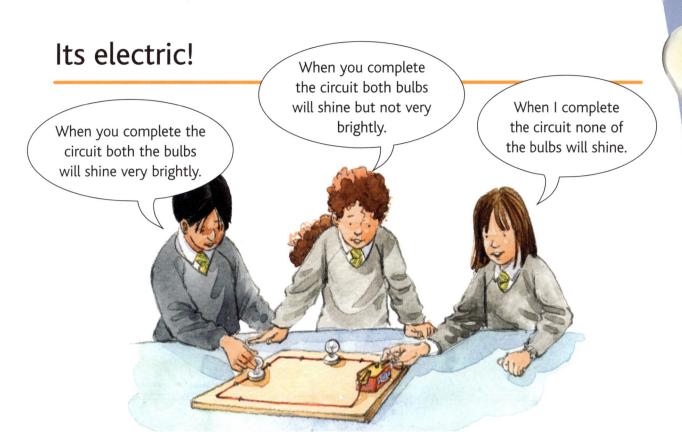

Who do you agree or disagree with? Why?

_____

_____

_____

Who do you agree or disagree with? Why?

_____

_____

_____

It's electric!

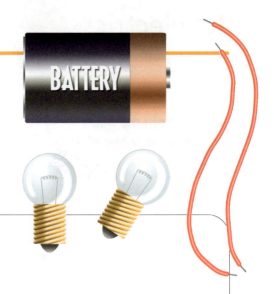

1   Make a simple circuit using one bulb, one bulb holder, two wires and one battery. Connect a second bulb to your circuit (you can use one more piece of wire). Draw a diagram of the second circuit.

2   Do the two bulbs shine as brightly as the single bulb did?

_____

3   Remove one of the bulbs from its holder. What happens? Why do you think this happens?

_____

_____

? **Did you know?**

This type of circuit is called a series circuit. There is only one path for the electric current to flow. The two bulbs are sharing the energy from the battery. When you remove one bulb the path is broken and the electric current cannot flow.

It's electric!

1 Arrange the two bulbs using the same battery so that they will both shine as brightly as the single bulb did in your first circuit. (You will need extra wire). If you unscrew one bulb the other should remain lighting. The battery should only have one wire coming from each terminal.

2 Draw a diagram of this circuit.

? Did you know?

In a parallel circuit the bulbs shine with equal brightness. Each bulb gets the full voltage from the battery. When you take one bulb out the other bulb will stay lighting because they each have their own circuit.

Batteries

Batteries store energy. This energy pushes the electric current around the circuit. The amount of energy in a battery is measured in **volts** (V). The higher the voltage the stronger the 'push' of energy. The number written on a battery tells you the voltage. The word volt comes from Alessandro Volto who invented the first battery in 1794.

It's electric!

Choose one of the switches you made. Draw a diagram of the switch in a circuit.

1 How did you make it?

_____

_____

2 Was it easy or difficult to make? Why?

_____

_____

3 What could your switch be used for?

_____

_____

It's electric!

Make an **electromagnet** like this one.

You will need
- paper clips
- a large nail
- 60cm of insulated wire
- a battery

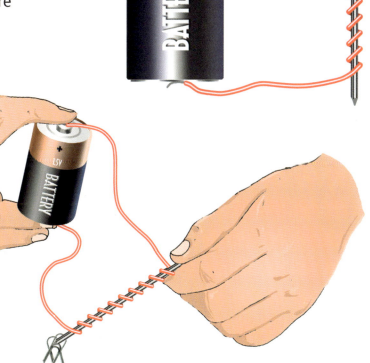

What to do
- Touch the nail to some paperclips. Does the nail attract them?

_____

- Wind the wire in one direction around the nail.
- Leave about 15cm of wire free at each end. Tape the ends.
- Connect each end of the wire to the battery.
- Will the nail pick up the paperclips now? Disconnect the wire from the battery.

Describe what happens?

_____
_____
_____

Investigate how you could make your electromagnet pick up more paper clips.

It's electric!

Draw the inside of a plug. Label the parts.

Describe the function of each part.

_____

_____

_____

_____

_____

_____

It's electric!

Safety in electricity

Electricity is a very useful source of energy. Mains electricity supply homes, schools and workplaces with power. Electricity is extremely useful and very powerful. It can be dangerous however, and must be used carefully.

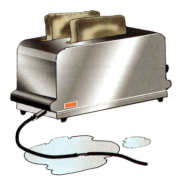
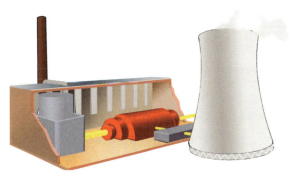

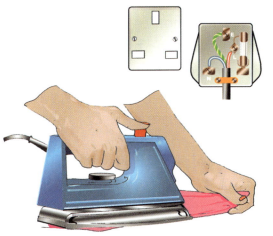

Here is a list of some safety rules.

1 Never ever touch mains electricity.

2 Do not overload sockets.

3 Do not use appliances near water.

4 Make sure plugs are correctly wired.

Can you add to the list?

_____

_____

_____

_____

_____

_____

Do some research

What else can you find out about electricity? Look up websites and books to find out more about electricity and electrical safety. Give a presentation to your class about interesting facts you have discovered.

Heating and insulating homes

Keeping the heat in

In cold weather we heat our homes. Homes should be heated to about 20°C. We waste energy and pay large heating bills when we overheat our homes. We can use energy wisely and save money by insulating our homes to keep the heat in. Some houses have wall cavity **insulation**. The gap between the inside and outside walls is filled with a thermal insulator to keep the heat in.

Many houses have attic insulation. This insulation reduces the upward flow of heat and keeps the inside of your home warm.

Most homes have a hot press. This is where the hot water is stored in a tank. To keep the water hot for as long as possible, the hot water tank should be insulated with a lagging jacket.

Some houses have double-glazed windows. Double-glazing is two panes of glass with a gap filled with air between. Air is a good thermal insulator. In some very cold climates, windows are triple-glazed!

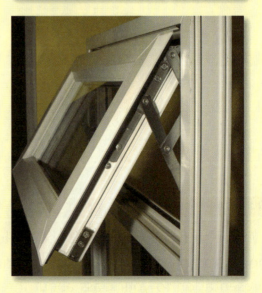

Heating and insulating homes

Look at these household objects. Are they thermal insulators or **conductors**?

Object	Material	Why is this material used?	Thermal insulator	Thermal conductor
plastic electric kettle				
heavy curtains				
cork table mat				
woollen blanket				
oven gloves				
glass dish				
wooden spoon				

Heating and insulating homes

Investigating house insulation.

House 1	House 2	House 3	House 4

No insulation	Insulation in the wall cavity only	Insulation in the roof only	Insulation in the roof and wall cavity

House and type of insulation	°C at start	°C after 2 mins	°C after 4 mins	°C after 6 mins	°C after 8 mins	°C after 10 mins	Drop in temp after 10 mins
1 House with with no insulation							
2 House with wall cavity insulation only							
3 House with roof insulation only							
4 House with roof and wall cavity insulation							

Heating and insulating homes

1 Which type of insulation was best? Why?

_____

_____

_____

_____

2 What was the drop in temperature in house 2 after ten minutes?

_____

3 Which house showed the biggest drop in temperature?

_____

_____

4 Why do you think this happened?

_____

_____

_____

5 Is it better to fit roof or wall cavity insulation?

_____

_____

_____

6 Is it better to fit both? Why?

_____

_____

_____

7 Predict the temperature of each house if you continued the investigation for another two minutes.

House 1 _____

House 2 _____

House 3 _____

House 4 _____

Have a heart

The circulatory system

The heart is a large muscle about the size of your clenched fist. It is found between the lungs in your chest. The heart is a pump which pushes blood continuously around your body.

The heart is part of the circulatory system. This system carries blood around our bodies. The blood contains food, oxygen and waste materials. The blood is carried around our bodies in tubes called blood vessels. There are two types of blood vessels. These are called arteries and veins.

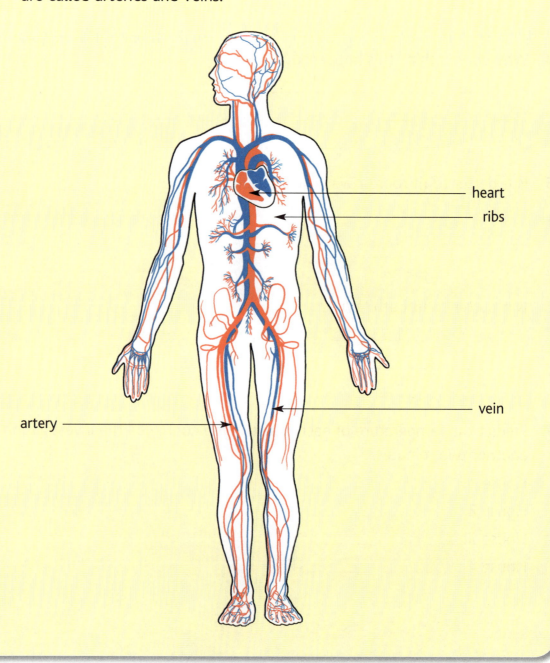

heart

ribs

vein

artery

Have a heart

The heart

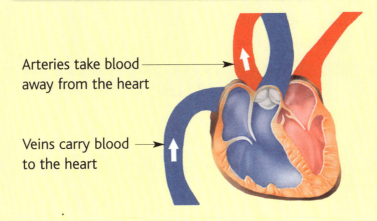

Arteries take blood away from the heart

Veins carry blood to the heart

The right-hand side of the heart is separated from the left-hand side by a wall made of muscle. The right-hand side receives blood from the body that contains carbon dioxide. The heart pumps this blood to the lungs. The left-hand side of the heart receives blood that has come from the lungs. This blood contains oxygen. Veins bring the blood into the heart and arteries carry blood away from the heart.

We can make sure we keep our hearts healthy by exercising, not eating too many fatty foods, and eating plenty of fruit and vegetables. Smoking damages the heart. It blocks the blood vessels and makes it difficult for the blood to pass through them. This puts pressure on the heart to keep pumping the blood around. Sometimes the heart is put under too much pressure and this can cause a heart attack.

Have a heart

Did you know?

You can feel your heart pumping blood around your body. You can detect your heartbeat by taking your pulse. This is the movement in the arteries as blood is pumped through them by the beating of the heart. You can take your pulse when an artery is close to the skin, for example at your wrist, temple or neck. Your heart beats about 70 times a minute when you are resting.

Try this

1 a Take your pulse three times and record your findings on the table below. Find your average pulse rate. Find the average pulse rate of the rest of your group in the same way. Record the results here.

Pulse rate per minute Name	1st reading	2nd reading	3rd reading	Average pulse rate

b Are all your pulse rates the same?

_____

c Whose pulse rate is faster than yours?

_____

d Whose pulse rate is slower than yours?

_____

Mixing, separating and other changes

Explore how metals rust.

You will need

- four saucers or shallow containers
- four nails
- salt and water solution
- petroleum jelly (Vaseline)
- water

What to do

- Place a nail in the saucer of salty water.
- Place a nail covered with petroleum jelly in the saucer of water.
- Place a nail covered with petroleum jelly in the saucer of salty water.
- Place a nail on the dry saucer.

Leave the saucers on a window sill and observe after a week.
Predict which nails will go rusty. Give reasons for your answer.

_____

_____

_____

_____

Our results

Saucer 1 _____

Saucer 2 _____

Saucer 3 _____

Saucer 4 _____

Give advice to someone who has just bought a vintage car. How can they keep it rust-free?

_____

_____

_____

_____

Mixing, separating and other changes

Record the burning times for each jar and calculate the average time.

Jar size	Trial 1	Trial 2	Trial 3	Average time
small				
medium				
large				

I think the flame burned longer in the _____ jar because

_____

_____

Draw a graph to show your results.

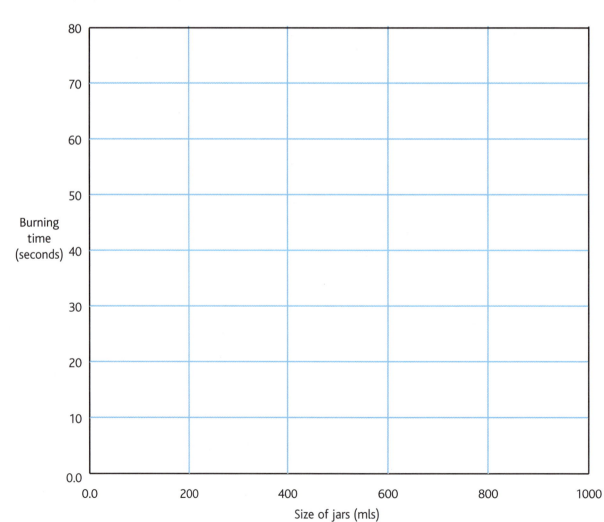

Habitats

A bluebell wood

Bluebells begin to grow in early spring before the leaves on the trees above have opened.
As they grow bluebells make food in their leaves.
This food is stored underground in the bulb.
When the leaves die, no more food is made until the plant grows new leaves the following spring.

Habitats

Describe the conditions of the habitats where these plants and animals are found.
Describe how each one is adapted to its environment.

1 Habitat

_____

Conditions of habitat

_____

_____

How the bluebell is adapted

_____

_____

2 Habitat

_____

Conditions of habitat

_____

_____

How the snail is adapted

_____

_____

3 Habitat

_____

Conditions of habitat

_____

_____

How the seaweed is adapted

_____

_____

4 Habitat

_____

Conditions of habitat

_____

_____

How the earthworm is adapted

_____

_____

Habitats

Let's talk.

Habitats

Food chains

A food chain shows how living things in a habitat depend on each other. A food chain begins with the sun and a plant.

Producer   Prey   Predator

Plants use the energy from sunlight to make food.
Plants are producers of food.
An animal that eats plants is a herbivore and a consumer (because he eats or consumes plants).
An animal that eats another animal is a carnivore and also a consumer (because he eats or consumes other animals).
An animal that is eaten by another animal is called the prey.
An animal that eats another animal is called the predator.

Producer   Herbivore consumer   Carnivore consumer

Choose three food chains from the hedgerow habitat to complete the following exercise.

_____   _____   _____

Producer ➜   herbivore consumer ➜   carnivore consumer

_____   _____   _____

Producer ➜   herbivore consumer ➜   carnivore consumer

_____   _____   _____

Producer ➜   herbivore consumer ➜   carnivore consumer

Habitats

New bypass planned

A new road to bypass the congested little village of Baile Álainn has been given the thumbs up. The new road will cut through Frog's Leap. It was hoped that this area would become a special area of conservation (SAC) as it is home to many animals and plants and an area of natural beauty. The road plans, while pleasing the villagers, are sure to upset many nature lovers.

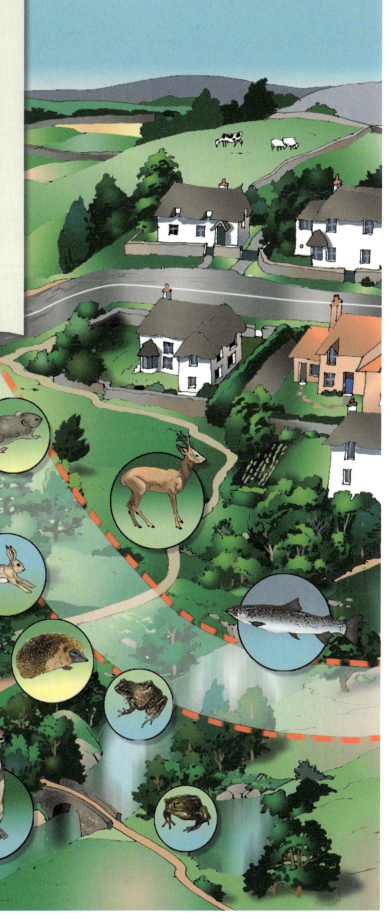

Light matters

Mixing the colours of light.

Plan how you are going to mix the colours of light.

_____

_____

_____

_____

_____

My results

_____

_____

_____

_____

Draw a diagram of your experiment showing the colours that were made.

What are the primary colours of light?

_____   _____   _____

Light matters

Design a coin trick.

You will need

- a coin
- a small piece of Blue-tac
- a margarine tub
- water

What to do

- Stick the coin to the inside bottom of the tub using the Blue-tac.
- Put the tub on a table.
- Look at the coin.
- Move your head backwards until the coin just disappears from view.
- Keep your head in this position and ask a your partner to slowly pour water into the container.

1 What happened when water was poured in to the container?

_____

_____

_____

_____

_____

_____

_____

2 Why did you think this happened?

_____

_____

_____

_____

_____

_____

_____

_____

Light matters

Bending light using a straw, a glass and water.

1 Put a straw into an empty glass.

2 Pour some water into the glass.

3 Draw a diagram of how your straw looks.

What did you notice?

_____

_____

_____

Why do you think this happened?

_____

_____

_____

 Did you know?

Light travels more slowly through water and glass than it does through air. When a ray of light hits the surface of water, it slows down and changes direction a little. The light ray looks as if has bent where it hits the water. This is called refraction.

In the coin activity when the rays of light hit the water in the container, they bent a little allowing you to see the coin.

When you experimented with the straw activity the rays of light hit the water in the glass and they changed direction. This made the straw look as if it was bent.

Light matters

Investigating lenses.

Try out each activity and record your results.

1 What shape is the magnifier?

_____

_____

_____

_____

Hold the magnifier over some newsprint. What do you notice?

_____

_____

_____

_____

2 Put two magnifiers together and hold them over some newsprint. What do you notice?

_____

_____

_____

_____

3 Find a lens that has a different shape to a magnifier. What shape is it?

_____

What happens when you place it over some newsprint?

_____

_____

_____

_____

4 What happens when you look at newsprint through a glass marble?

_____

_____

_____

_____

Light matters

Lenses

Transparent materials such as glass and water can work as **lenses**. You have a lens in each eye. Muscles pull on the lens in your eye to make it fat or thin. When you look at things close-up, your lens grows fat. Your lens becomes thinner to view things far away.

Lenses are curved on one or both sides and are useful for bending light in special ways.

Lenses make objects look larger or smaller depending on their shape.

Lenses are used in glasses, cameras microscopes and telescopes.

A microscope uses several sets of lenses and can make tiny objects look hundreds or thousands of times bigger.

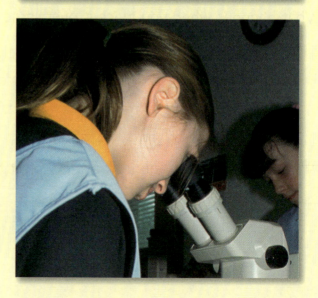

How plants reproduce

Parts of a plant

The leaf makes food through the process of photosynthesis. It allows oxygen in and carbon dioxide out.

The flower makes seeds during reproduction.

The stem holds the leaves, flowers and fruit. It carries water and minerals from the roots up through the plant. It carries food made in the leaves up and down the plant.

Roots anchor the plant in the ground. They absorb water and minerals from the soil. The roots of some plants such as carrots and turnips can store food.

Parts of a plant

How plants reproduce

Examine the tulip. Describe the leaf.

_____

_____

_____

Draw the leaf here.

Describe the petals.

_____

_____

_____

Find a circle of tall thin parts inside the petals. These are the stamens. How many stamens can you see?

_____

What colour are they?

_____

Touch the top of one of them. Does any powder come off on your fingers? This powder is called pollen.

How plants reproduce

Look at the part of the flower that sticks up in the middle.
This is called the pistil. What colour is it?

_____

What shape is it?

_____

Draw a diagram of the flower here. Name as many parts as you can.

How plants reproduce

How flowers reproduce

- Each part of the flower plays an important part in the reproduction of the flowering plant.

- The petals are coloured and the flowers are scented to attract visiting insects.

- The stamens are the male parts of the flower.

- The pistil is the female part of the flower.

- The flowering plant reproduces by a process called pollination.
- During pollination, the male part of the flower produces pollen. The pollen grains are blown by the wind or carried by insects to the pistil in the female part of the flower. There they fuse with the egg cell in the ovary to form a new seed.

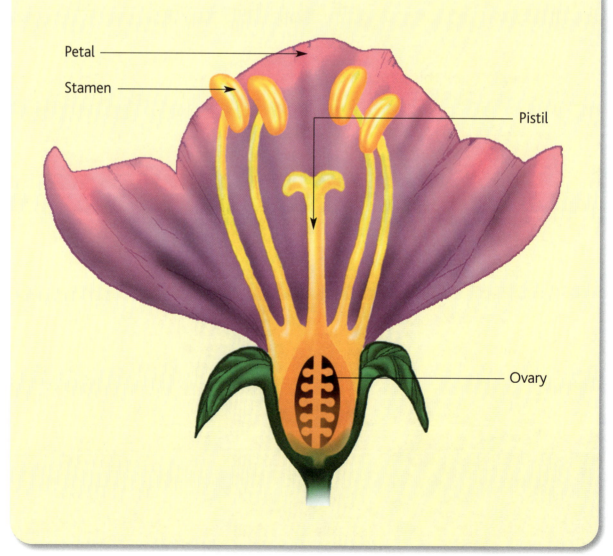

Petal

Stamen

Pistil

Ovary

Under pressure

Air exerts pressure.

1 What happened when you hit the ruler?

_____

_____

_____

Why do you think this happened?

_____

_____

_____

2 What happened to the carton when you sucked the air out?

_____

_____

_____

Why do you think this happened?

_____

_____

_____

3 What happened when you turned the jar upside down?

_____

_____

_____

Why do you think this happened?

_____

_____

_____

Under pressure

? **Did you know?**

A **pneumatic system** uses air pressure to make things move ('pneumatic' comes from the Greek word 'pneuma' for breath). Air can be compressed (squashed) into a smaller space. This increases its pressure. The compressed air in these pneumatic systems pushes out with enough force to raise the objects.

Make your own pneumatic systems.

What you need

- two sandwich bags
- plastic tubing
- sellotape
- one copy book

What to do

- Tape a plastic bag to the end of a piece of tubing. Inflate the bag by blowing into it.
- Squeeze the tube so the bag stays inflated.
- Tape a second bag to the other end of the tubing.

  1 Squeeze the first bag. What happened?

  _____

  2 Squeeze the second bag. What happened?

  _____

! **Try this**

- Attach a sandwich bag to the plastic tubing.
- Place a copybook on the bag.
- Blow into the tubing.

  1 What happened to the book?

  _____

  _____

  2 Add more books to the pile. How many copybooks can you lift using your pneumatic system?

  _____

Under pressure

This is another type of pneumatic system. Put it together and answer the questions below.

You will need
- two syringes
- plastic tubing

What to do
- Attach a syringe to either end of the plastic tubing.

1 Push one of the syringes. What happened?

_____

_____

2 Push the other syringe. What happened?

_____

_____

3 What do you think makes the syringes move each time?

_____

_____

_____

_____

Under pressure

Discuss these different pneumatic systems.

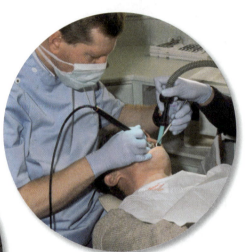

Do some research!

Research and describe one of these systems and how it works.

_____

_____

_____

_____

_____

_____

_____

_____

_____

_____

Under pressure

Experimenting with water pressure.

What you need

- large plastic bottle
- Blue-tac or plasticine
- water
- tray or newspaper

What to do

- Make three holes down the side of the plastic bottle about 4cm apart. Cover each hole with Blue-tac or plasticine.

- Fill the bottle with water. Place it on a tray or newspaper.

- Remove the bottom piece of Blue-tac and observe how far the water shoots out. Measure and record the distance on the table.

- Put the Blue-tac back over the bottom hole, refill the bottle. Remove the Blue-tac from the bottom two holes and observe how far the water shoots out of the middle hole. Measure and record the distance on the table.

- Refill the bottle and remove all three pieces of Blue-tac. Observe how far the water shoots out of the top hole. Measure and record the distance on the table.

How far the water shot out from each hole	
bottom hole	
middle hole	
top hole	

Why do you think this happened?

_____

_____

_____

_____

Under pressure

Make your own hydraulic system.

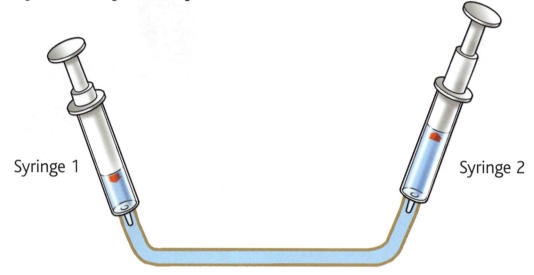

Syringe 1   Syringe 2

You will need

• two syringes   • plastic tubing   • water   • basin

What to do

• Attach the syringes to either end of the tubing.

• Take the middle sections (pistons) out of the syringes and put the syringes and tubing into the basin of water.

• While the syringes are still under water push one piston fully into syringe 1. Put the other piston slightly into syringe 2.

• Take the tube and syringes out of the water. Push the piston in syringe 2 fully into the syringe.

1 What happened to the piston in syringe 1?

_____

2 Why do you think this happened?

_____

3 Push the piston in syringe 1 fully into the syringe. What happened?

_____

? **Did you know?**

A **hydraulic system** uses water pressure to make things move. If you press one part of the liquid, the pressure increases throughout and the liquid has to move somewhere else.

Under pressure

Discuss these hydraulic systems.

Discuss how wind and water energy is used.

More about plants and animals

Describing plants.

Draw and label a diagram of four plants. Write a description of each.

More about plants and animals

Animal groups.

Hold a brainstorm about your animal group. Write the name of the group in the centre of the diagram and record what you know about them.

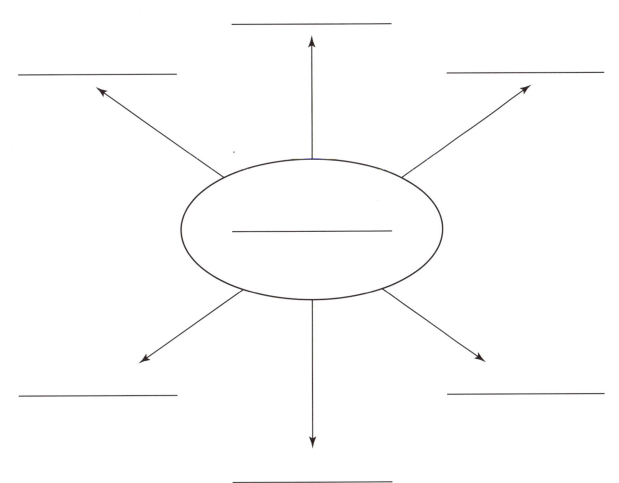

! **Do some research**

Research your animal group. Record your information here.

_____

_____

_____

_____

_____

_____

_____

_____

Glossary

conductor
material that is good at letting heat energy pass through it

digestive system
where food we eat is broken down into tiny pieces so they can be taken around our body by the blood

electromagnet
a soft metal made into a magnet by passing an electric current through a wire surrounding it

hydraulic system
uses water pressure to make things move

insulate
stop the passage of heat energy or electricity

lens
a piece of curved, transparent material used to bend light

mass
how much matter or material is contained by something

pitch
how high or low a sound is

pneumatic system
containing or operated by compressed air

vibrate
to move back and forward rapidly

volt
a unit for measuring electrical force

weight
how heavy something is